DIG AND DISCOVER CRYSTALS

by Anita Nahta Amin

T0053121

CAPSTONE PRESS
a capstone imprint

Published by Capstone Press, an imprint of Capstone
1710 Roe Crest Drive, North Mankato, Minnesota 56003
capstonepub.com

Library of Congress Cataloging-in-Publication Data is available on the Library of
Congress website
ISBN: 9781666342444 (hardcover)
ISBN: 9781666342468 (paperback)
ISBN: 9781666342475 (ebook PDF)

Summary: Crystals can be rare and valuable or common and even edible! Uncover
how crystals form and where you can search for them.

All internet sites appearing in back matter were available and accurate when this
book was sent to press.

DISCLAIMER:

This book provides information about various types of rocks and where and how to find them. Before
entering any area in search of rocks, make sure that the area is open to the public or that you have secured
permission from the property owner to go there. Also, take care not to damage any property, and do not
remove any rocks from the area unless you have permission to do so.

Rock hunting in riverbeds, quarries, mines, and some of the other areas identified in this book can be
inherently risky. You should not engage in any of these activities without parental supervision. Also, you
should always wear proper safety equipment and know how to use any tools that you bring with you. You
should not engage in any activity that is beyond your ability or skill or comfort level. Failure to follow
these guidelines may result in damage to property or serious injury or death to you or others, and may
also result in substantial civil or criminal liability.

The publisher and the author shall not be liable for any damages allegedly arising from the information
in this book, and they specifically disclaim any liability from the use or application of any of the contents
of this book.

Printed and bound in the USA. 4882

CONTENTS

Words in **bold** are in the glossary.

INTRODUCTION
WHAT A FIND!

Imagine sifting through rocks at a mine. Suddenly, a sparkle catches your eye. You pick out a small, clear stone. It's a crystal! But what kind? You study it and look in your guidebook. It's topaz! This is your first find as a **rock hound**. After recording the find in your log, you store the crystal. You will clean it later. Right now, there are more crystals to find!

Crystals can be found all over the world. You see them in jewelry. Many people collect them as a hobby.

You can collect crystals too! But where do you find them? How do you identify them? Let's find out!

Sometimes you can find crystals,
such as topaz, jutting out of rocks.

FACT

People even collected crystals 105,000 years ago! A
collection of calcite crystals was found in an ancient
rock shelter in Africa.

CHAPTER 1
ANCIENT BEAUTY

A red ruby from a mango grove in India. A white diamond from a mine in Russia. A pale blue aquamarine from the Blue Ridge Mountains. All over the world, crystals are waiting to be found. They hide in mountains, in streams, and underground.

When you pick up a crystal, it might be millions of years old! This makes crystals important to scientists. They can learn how Earth looked back then. Different kinds of crystals form in different climates and regions. Scientists can see how hot Earth was in the past and if water was present. Scientists even study space crystals to learn about other planets and moons.

Rubies are especially common in Myanmar.

FACT

A zircon found in Jack Hills, Australia, is the oldest known crystal in the world. It is 4.375 billion years old!

Certain minerals, such as bismuth, can form detailed crystal patterns.

Is It a Rock?

Rocks are made of a blend of **minerals**. Granite is a rock. It has minerals such as quartz and feldspar. There are more than 5,000 minerals in nature. Quartz and feldspar are two of the most common on Earth.

Many minerals form crystals. A crystal is a physical structure. Crystals are solid like rocks. But crystals are made of atoms that repeat in a pattern. Atoms are tiny building blocks too small to see. Imagine stacking the same kind of blocks over and over again. This is how a crystal is made!

Crystals don't come from only minerals, though. They also come from materials that are alive or were once living. But mineral crystals are the type rock hounds collect.

FACT

Microscopic creatures in California's Mono Lake let out hazenite crystals. They release the crystals when the lake they live in dries up. Hazenite is found only in this desert lake.

Some crystals grow near hot springs.

Growing Up

Some crystals are too small to see without a microscope. Others are taller than you! How does this happen?

Melted rock like lava and liquids in hot springs are rich in minerals. Gases can be too. As they cool, crystals grow. You might find quartz near hot springs or diamonds in volcanic rock.

Each kind of crystal needs the right temperature and pressure to start and keep growing. The right conditions let mineral atoms move and join others nearby. The crystal grows as more atoms attach. Some crystals grow only in certain regions with certain minerals.

Crystals form when liquids dry up too. Minerals stay behind and stick together to form crystals. Salt water dries up, leaving halite, or salt.

Crystals need time and space to grow. Without space, crystals grow into each other. When conditions change, a crystal might stop growing.

FACT

The Cave of Crystals in Mexico has some of the largest crystals in the world. The gypsum beams are up to 36 feet (11 meters) long and weigh up to 55 tons. That is more than three times taller than a school bus and as heavy as eight male African bush elephants!

CHAPTER 2
PERFECT OR NOT

Are you ready to find the perfect crystal? There are a few things to look for. A perfect crystal has symmetry. This means both halves look the same. It has smooth sides called faces. And it forms **geometric** shapes.

A crystal's shape is based on how the atoms join together. The same type of atoms can form different kinds of crystals. The graphite in pencil lead has the same kind of atoms as diamonds.

Oops!

Most crystals aren't perfect. They may have some atoms missing from their structure. This can change the crystal's color. For example, pure fluorite is colorless. But missing atoms can give it a purple color.

Sugar can form fairly symmetrical crystals.

Atoms that don't belong might join. These **impurities** can make patterns on the crystal. A cat's eye is a line of impurities shining in the light. More than one cat's eye in the crystal make a star. Sometimes, the crystal on one side of the cat's eye looks lighter than the other. This is called milk and honey.

FACT FILE

Name: crystal

Size: microscopic to many feet long

Time to grow: minutes to millions of years

Kinds: There are more than 5,000 kinds of minerals. Most form crystals, and many can form more than one kind of crystal. Material that is alive or was once living can sometimes make crystals too.

Found: all over the world in rocks, sand, streams, underground, near hot springs and volcanoes, and more

Varieties: Many crystals come in different colors or patterns, including cat's eye, star, and milk and honey.

Shape: geometric

Luster: dull, silky, vitreous (glass-like), metallic, resinous (like amber and other tree resins), greasy, adamantine (the brightest luster), or earthy (like dry mud)

Impurities can change a crystal's color too. Corundum is normally colorless. Different impurities give it color. A red corundum is a ruby. Blue makes it a sapphire. These are both gems. A gem is a precious stone or crystal, often set in jewelry. It gets its value from being rare, long lasting, and pretty.

CHAPTER 3
GET READY FOR A TREASURE HUNT!

The hunt for crystals is on! Maybe you'll find quartz or even a diamond! It could be as easy as stepping outside and looking down. Or it could be as hard as cracking a geode, a type of hollow rock with crystals inside.

First decide the type of collection you want. Do you want to collect only certain kinds of crystals? Or colors? Maybe you want crystals from only a certain region. Or maybe you want everything you can find. It's up to you! But deciding will help you know where to look.

Rockhounding is a fun
way to experience nature.

Mountainous areas can have crystals waiting to be discovered.

Road Trip!

Streams, mountains, and old volcanic regions are good places to start looking. Ask an adult to check your state's **geology** department online. These organizations often list public rockhounding places.

You could also join a geology club. Many clubs take field trips to find rocks. Some places are open only to club members.

Some quarries and mines are open to the public for a fee. Emerald Hollow Mine in North Carolina lets you look for emeralds. Crater of Diamonds State Park in Arkansas lets you keep the diamonds you find. Gem Mountain in Montana has sapphires. Cherokee Ruby and Sapphire Mine in North Carolina has rubies and sapphires.

Fantastic Find!

In March 2017, 14-year-old Kalel Langford was tired from a baseball game. But he really wanted to find a diamond. After less than 30 minutes of looking in Crater of Diamonds State Park in Arkansas, he got his wish. It had rained recently, and now he saw a 7.44-**carat** brown diamond near a stream! Kalel named his find Superman's Diamond. It was the seventh-largest diamond ever found there.

Many people enjoy searching for diamonds at Crater of Diamonds State Park.

Certain tools and equipment can help you safely find crystals.

Gear Up!

A storm may uncover some crystals on the ground. But most are buried in dirt or rock. You will need a small shovel.

A geology hammer from a hardware store can break small rocks. Don't use a regular hammer. It can break and hurt you. You may need a chisel to carve out a crystal. An adult should help with both of these tools.

The proper gear will help you dig up your crystal and keep it from getting damaged.

Fantastic Find!

In 1820, Elijah Hamlin and a friend from college were hiking on Mount Mica in Maine. When they took a break, Elijah found a green crystal under a tree. It turned out to be tourmaline. The hill was covered with it! Elijah was the first person to find tourmaline in the United States. This led to the opening of the first gem mine in the nation.

Selenite crystals can break easily.

You'll need something to carry your treasures. A pail can hold dirt and rocks to look through later. Keep fragile crystals, such as needlelike selenite, safe in an empty egg carton.

Above all, stay safe! Wear safety glasses and a helmet. Closed-toe shoes, gloves, long-sleeve shirts, and pants can protect you from sharp rocks. Carry a compass in unfamiliar places so you don't get lost. Always rockhound with an adult.

Follow the Rules!

Do your research before you hunt for crystals. Some places don't allow rockhounding. Other sites, like wildlife refuges, limit when and where you can dig. Some places, like national forests, limit what you can keep or sell afterward. A fee or permit may be needed. To dig on private property, you must have the owner's permission.

Follow the site's rules to stay safe. Never go into abandoned mines, tunnels, or flooded quarries. Don't go into streams or rivers. Don't work under ledges where loose rock can fall on you. If you dig a hole, fill it in so no one trips.

CHAPTER 4
WHICH CRYSTAL IS IT?

So you've found a crystal! But what kind is it? Ask an adult to help you compare your results with online tables and guidebooks. Many state geology websites show local crystals too.

Check the color. Some crystals are always the same color. Peridot is green. But other crystals may share that color. Then what?

A scratch test will narrow your choices, though it could damage your crystal. The Mohs hardness scale ranks crystals from soft to hard. If a penny can scratch your crystal, the crystal is soft. You can then narrow your research to soft crystals. A penny scratches soft calcite but not hard quartz.

A crystal's color, such as the green of peridot, is one of several clues to what type of crystal you have found.

Some crystals, such as garnet, contain iron. Magnets stick to iron. If a magnet sticks to your crystal, check your guidebook for crystals with iron.

Look at the luster. Is your crystal dull or shiny? How your crystal reflects light is a clue too.

Sometimes, even experts get confused! If you get stuck, see if your local museum or geology club can help.

CHAPTER 5
CARE FOR YOUR TREASURE

Your crystal may need a gentle cleaning. A **loupe** or magnifying glass will help you see better while cleaning. Use a soft toothbrush to remove dried-on dirt. Most common crystals can be washed with soapy water. But don't wash crumbly crystals or salts like halite. They will break apart. Don't wash crystals with iron in them either. They will rust.

If your crystal is hard and without pores, like quartz, it can be tumbled. A tumbler machine polishes crystals by spinning or shaking them with grit and water. Only tumble crystals with a Mohs hardness between 5 and 8. Softer crystals like calcite will crumble in a tumbler. It can take more than a month to polish a crystal in a tumbler.

Gypsum crystals are among the crystals that are too soft to polish in a tumbler.

There are endless ways to display your crystals!

Record It!

A log will help you keep track of your collection. Use a notebook, index cards, or computer.

First, tag the crystal with a unique number. Paint a white dot of correction fluid on the bottom of the crystal. You can also use a sticker. Write the number on the dried correction fluid or sticker.

In your log, list the number and the kind of crystal. Include its size, color, and shape, and also when and where you found it. Many collectors add photos of their crystals. Log your crystal soon after finding it so you don't forget!

Store your crystals in a cool, dry place. Many collectors keep them in plastic or cardboard boxes. The crystals shouldn't touch. They might nick each other.

Then go out and rockhound again. Maybe you'll discover a rare crystal no one has seen before!

CRYSTAL CATALOG

NUMBER	DATE FOUND	CRYSTAL NAME	SIZE	COLOR	DESCRIPTION	LOCATION
1	August 7, 2022	diamond	9 x 5 x 2 mm	white	looks like a teardrop; has a black dot	Crater of Diamonds State Park, Arkansas, near the river
2	September 15, 2022	sunstone	3.5 x 3.2 x 1.7 mm	pale orange	triangular; white spot in corner looks like a maple leaf	Oregon Sunstone Public Collection Area

GLOSSARY

carat (KAR-uht)—a unit of weight for precious stones equal to 200 milligrams

geology (jee-AH-luh-jee)—the study of rocks and other materials that make up Earth

geometric (jee-uh-MET-rik)—having a regular shape, such as a square or triangle

impurity (im-PYOOR-ih-tee)—a substance that doesn't normally belong in a crystal

loupe (LOOP)—a special magnifier used by jewelers

luster (LUS-tur)—the way the surface of a mineral looks when reflecting light

mineral (MIN-ur-uhl)—a substance found in nature that is not made by a plant or animal

rock hound (ROK HAUND)—someone who looks for and collects rocks as a hobby